ESTATE PLANNING

Explained Simply and Done Right

Christopher L. Cauble, Esq.

Speakeasy Publishing
73-03 Bell Blvd, #10
Oakland Gardens, NY 11364
www.speakeasypublishinginc.com

Ordering Information:

Quantity sales. Special discounts are available on quantity purchases by corporations, associations, and others. For details, contact the publisher at the address above.

Orders by U.S. trade bookstores and wholesalers. Please contact Speakeasy Publishing: Tel: (888) 991-2766 or visit www.speakeasypublishinginc.com.

Printed in the United States of America.

Published in 2018

ISBN: 978-1-946481-58-0

PREFACE

This book is designed to provide information on estate planning in a simple to understand and comprehensive process. My firm has been doing estate planning for generations, and we have done work with all kinds of estates. I have also litigated estate matters, such as will contests and trust disputes. This gives me a good view as to what works and what does not work in estate plans, as well as pitfalls to avoid.

I hope that you enjoy this book and find it informative. Estate planning can be a difficult process and, hopefully, those who read this book will come away with a better understanding.

Dedication

This book is dedicated to my father, Walter, who has guided me through my law practice and my wife, Tracy, who continues to inspire me to be a better man.

DISCLAIMER

This publication is intended to be used for educational purposes only. No legal advice is being given, and no attorney-client relationship is intended to be created by reading this material. The author assumes no liability for any errors or omissions or for how this book or its contents are used or interpreted or for any consequences resulting directly or indirectly from the use of this book. For legal or any other advice, please consult an experienced attorney or the appropriate expert who is aware of the specific facts of your case and is knowledgeable of the law in your jurisdiction.

Cauble, Cauble & Selvig, LLP

111 S.E. 6th Street

Grants Pass, OR 97526

www.thecaublefirm.com

(541) 476-8825

TESTIMONIALS

"Chris has provided me with competent legal representation in both personal and business matters. He has represented me in court on several occasions where my case was presented in a factual and concise manner resulting in prevailing rulings under difficult circumstances. Juries listen to Chris because he routinely presents a case in a logical and easy to understand manner that is difficult to ignore. He is one attorney who listens and provides competent legal advice and takes appropriate action when necessary. I have known him for more than 10 years and have continued to use him because he is one of the best in this town."

- Martin

****

"I have been extremely pleased with the work Chris Cauble has done for me. He has worked very hard setting up my trust fund and working through my parents' very complicated trust. He has kept me informed every step of the way and always explained everything. I will continue to use him in the future, as he has my complete trust."

- Lee

****

"I have used Chris Cauble as my family attorney for many years. I have always found him to be very knowledgeable and professional in my dealings with him. He is a very helpful and caring person. It makes me feel more secure knowing that he is looking out for me. I would very highly recommend him to any person needing legal assistance."

- Anonymous

****

"I have worked with Chris Cauble on many legal issues and he is one of the most competent and professional attorneys in the community. He really cares about his clients and strives to provide the best service to them, whether it is working on their estate matters or representing them in the courtroom."

- Robert M.

****

TABLE OF CONTENTS

About The Author

Christopher Cauble's practice is located in a medium sized Oregon town, but his firm handles cases all over the state of Oregon regarding various types of litigation, in both Federal and State courts. He frequently associates with out-of-state law firms. He knows ins and outs of litigating in this state. His firm has been a fixture in Southern Oregon for over 50 years and is well known throughout the state for providing excellent legal services. Chris also does various types of transactional work, including estates and estate planning. He has a large and professional staff available to support his law firm and help the clients with their needs. He is lucky to live in a beautiful part of the Country and be able to translate his hard work ethic into results for his clients.

AREAS OF PRACTICE

- Complex Civil Litigation and Trial work In Federal and State Court
- Probate, Trusts and Estate Planning
- Real Estate and Transactions
- Water Law
- Appeals (Federal and State)
- Business Law, Litigation and Transactions

BAR ADMISSIONS

- Oregon, 1996
- U.S. District Court District of Oregon
- United States Tax Court
- 9th Circuit Court of Appeals
- United States Supreme Court

EDUCATION

- Gonzaga University School of Law, Spokane, Washington
- J.D. cum laude – 1996
- Willamette University, BA with Departmental Honors, 1993

HONORS AND AWARDS

- Super Lawyers, 2013
- 10 Best Law Firms-Oregon (Estate Planning)-American Institute of Legal Counsel
- Best Attorneys of America, 2015
- Better Business Bureau Small Business of the Year for Oregon, 2015

PROFESSIONAL ASSOCIATIONS AND MEMBERSHIPS

- Oregon State Bar Administrative Law Executive Committee, Chair, 2009
- Oregon State Bar House of Delegates, Member, 2000 - Present
- Oregon State Bar Ethics Committee, 2002 - 2005
- Oregon State Bar Judicial Administration Committee, 2006 - Present

- Oregon State Bar LPRC, 2006 - 2008

PRO BONO ACTIVITIES

- Rogue Gateway Rotary Club, President, 2006
- Grants Pass Scholarship Foundation Board of Directors, Vice President
- Rogue Community College Foundation Board of Directors
- Rogue Valley Chorale Association
- Boy Scouts of America, Board Member

CHAPTER 1

WHY DID YOU CHOOSE TO PRACTICE ESTATE PLANNING?

I grew up in Grants Pass, Oregon, and joined the same law firm as my father in 1996. The firm has a large estate planning practice that primarily handles probates and trust administration in Southern Oregon. In addition, the firm does litigation of trust and real estate disputes. I have been involved with estate planning and estate administration/probate since joining the firm.

We have a statewide practice in Oregon and a reputation for our work in estates and litigation. My motivation for writing this book, as well as my interest in estate planning in general, stems from the fact that so many things can go wrong when estate planning is not handled properly. It is my goal to ensure that people understand the basics of estate planning so that when they meet with an attorney, they will understand estate planning. I also want to dispel many of the rumors surrounding estate planning, trust administration, and probate.

I want to encourage clients to become more knowledgeable in terms of estate planning, and to identify their estate planning needs as they experience changes in life, including increases and decreases in wealth, changes within the family, and issues concerning wealth and retirement. I have seen how poor estate planning causes families to break up, leads to litigation, and can cost thousands of dollars as well as permanent damages in the family that could have been avoided. The goal is to avoid these consequences and make the process as simple as possible.

CHAPTER 2

WHAT IS ESTATE PLANNING?

Estate planning is the process of determining how to manage your assets during your lifetime and how to distribute them in the future. Everyone has an estate, and whether or not you like it, there are laws that kick in if you fail to properly and comprehensively prepare your estate correctly. Correct planning involves making sure that you have the correct documents prepared and the correct plan in place to ensure that your assets are administered and distributed in a way that protects your children from creditors, and other types of claims against your estate.

Estate planning also involves minimizing taxes during your life, as well as your death and, in certain circumstances, protecting yourself and your children from claims from creditors.

I consider estate planning to be a three-legged stool, involving proper legal, financial, and tax advice. This book is primarily meant to discuss the first tier, which I believe is the most important because it involves the drafting of wills, trusts, and advance directives (also known as healthcare powers of attorney in many states).

Why Do We Need Estate Plans? What Happens If I Die Without An Estate Plan Or Will?

If you die without an estate plan, then you will have lost control over what happens to your estate. Under such circumstances, state laws determine how your assets are to be distributed and who will act as the executor of your estate. If you have a will, then you will know who your executor is going to be and to whom your assets will be distributed. If you have a trust, then you will know who your trustee is going to be and how your assets will be distributed once you pass. In addition, you will be able to create a proper tax setup in your trust in order to ensure that state, federal, and gift taxes will be managed correctly.

If these measures are not taken and you have a significant estate, then you could end up having to pay taxes that you otherwise would not have had to pay. If you fail to create a will, then state law will determine where your assets will go, even if you wanted your assets to be distributed in a different way.

If you fail to create a trust and you become incapacitated, then there will not be a trustee to take over your estate if you are incapacitated or deceased. Instead, if you are still alive, the state could appoint a conservator to manage your property, which may not be what you would have wanted. Having a conservator appointed is expensive, time consuming, and can result in your assets being managed in a manner contrary to what you would have wanted.

Furthermore, if you have children who are disabled and subject to potential federal or state aid, and if you fail to do planning in a spendthrift trust or an asset protection trust, then those children could lose their federal or state benefits. There are many unintended consequences of improper estate planning.

CHAPTER 3

WHY DO PEOPLE AVOID OR DELAY ESTATE PLANS?

Many people have a hard time envisioning and planning for their death, in part because it is psychologically very difficult to do. In addition, many people believe that they cannot afford estate planning, or that it is only for people who are very wealthy. That, however, is simply not true; everyone needs to do some measure of planning for their estate, whether it is a simple will or a complex trust. While there are certainly costs associated with estate planning, they are not prohibitive and certainly outweigh the consequences of foregoing planning altogether.

Oftentimes, people will avoid making an estate plan if there are difficulties related to the family dynamic, or indecision about how to handle their estate. For instance, if there is a child who predeceased the parent, a child who became estranged from the family, or there are no children at all, then they might not know to whom to give their estate, and this is somewhat common.

If someone becomes mentally incompetent to create their will or trust, then whatever they had at the time of becoming incompetent basically becomes frozen in place. For example, they might have an estate plan that is 20 or 30 years old or a will that they've had since being in the military, and if that estate plan or will has not been updated, then it may not be effective for their current financial situation. If the tax laws have changed since they drafted their trust, then it too will need to be updated. It is kind of like going to the dentist; no one wants to and most people avoid it for as long as they can, but if they never go, then their teeth will eventually become severely damaged and they will be facing more pain than they would have, had they just gone to the dentist in the first place.

CHAPTER 4

HOW OFTEN SHOULD I GIVE MY ESTATE PLAN A CHECKUP?

You should give your estate plan a checkup if a substantial event has occurred, such as a divorce, remarriage, a death in the family, or a significant increase or decrease in wealth. Divorce is an important event that requires someone to update their estate plan, because in most states, any distributions to a spouse that were in place before the divorce are automatically revoked. That does not necessarily revoke the whole estate plan, but you may find that there are some unintended consequences of doing that.

For example, you may want to ensure that your stepchildren still receive some of your assets. If you remarry, then you will want to speak with an attorney about how to restructure your estate plan based upon that new marriage and any subsequent marriages. If there has been a death in the family, you would want to make changes so that person's share of assets goes to someone else. Lastly, it is important to update your estate plan if your financial situation has changed, because you may become subject to a federal or state tax issue that could be minimized through trust planning.

If no substantial events have occurred in your life, then you should give your estate plan a checkup every 10 years. Most attorneys will send checkup letters every 10 years to remind people to look at their trusts or wills and determine whether or not they need to make changes. Typically, we do not have to redo the entire trust document, but there are usually enough changes that need to be made to justify changing the entire trust document or will.

CHAPTER 5

PARTIES INVOLVED IN AN ESTATE PLAN

In the case of a trust, a trustor (or Grantor), trustee and beneficiary(ies) will be involved,

The trustee is the person who will manage the estate, and the grantor is the person who creates and funds the trust. Typically, you will actually be the trustee as well as the grantor when you first create the trust. We will set up alternate or successor trustees who can automatically take control of the trust once you pass, decide to resign as trustee, or become incapacitated and unable to act as trustee. The beneficiaries to an estate plan will also be involved, because they will benefit from the trust after you pass or after certain events occur. There can be current beneficiaries, meaning that you can have a trust for someone and currently provide for them as well. Alternatively, there can be people who will become beneficiaries only once you pass away.

In the case of a will, a "testator" or "testatrix" will be involved. These are terms that define the maker of the will. In addition, a personal representative or the executor of the will is the person who is appointed in the will to act as the executor of the estate, meaning that they will file the necessary documents with the court in order to start the probate process. Executors ensure that the terms of the will are followed, that the taxes, final bills of the estate, and final burial expenses are paid, and that everything else gets taken care of. This is all done under court supervision, as most states require judges to sign off on all major steps of the probate process.

Outside of a trust or will, there will be the lawyers who will draft the documents, help you to manage or administer the trust or will, and deal with any disputes that may arise. In most cases, you will have an attorney help you draft the documents for probate, go through the probate process itself, represent you in court (if any court hearings are necessary), and complete the final account. You may have accountants who will assist you with filing your tax returns during the trust administration or probate process. In addition, you may have some financial advisers who will help you decide how to manage your assets in the trust, how to invest your money in order to maximize your wishes in the trust, how to best provide for the beneficiaries, and how to ensure that taxes and maximum investment advantages are addressed.

CHAPTER 6

MEASURES FOR INCAPACITY IN AN ESTATE PLAN

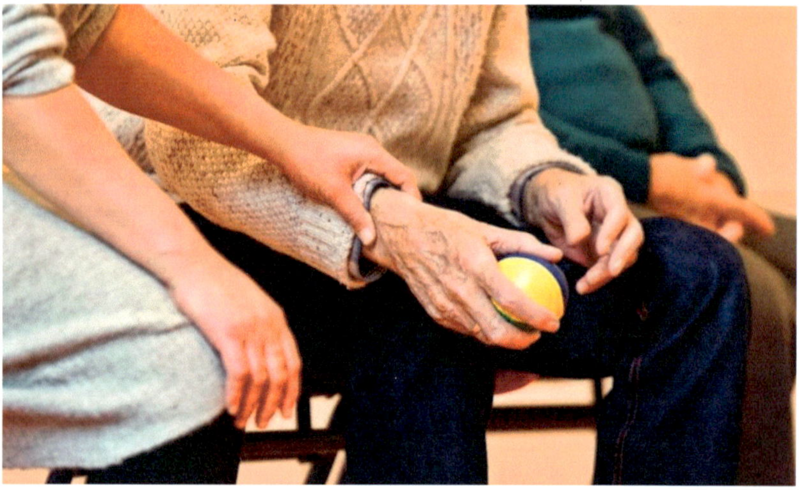

Most people include measures for incapacity in their estate plans. In fact, if you have a questionable level of competency or capacity to create a trust, then every responsible attorney will conduct a test in order to determine whether or not you have the capacity to make decisions regarding the trust. In most states, the level of capacity to do a trust is not extremely high, but does require that you understand what property you have, acknowledge your intention to create a will or trust, identify your beneficiaries, understand the documents that you will be required to sign, and be generally cognizant of the time and location.

It is important to establish capacity because if there is a dispute in the future concerning your capacity, then you will have an attorney or a witness who has already performed a test in order to determine your capacity. Having had that test conducted will make it very difficult for anyone to challenge your trust or will based on capacity. Very infrequently we will encounter someone who does not have the capacity to do a trust. However, this isn't only because they are forgetful or have some difficulty with their finances. An incapacitated person must be completely unaware of their circumstances, their property, and basic concepts of the documents they are signing.

In many cases, you may be suffering from some sort of advanced dementia or other physical condition. However, you have a basic understanding of what a trust and will do and how your decisions will impact your family and assets. In this case, you are able to sign a trust or will and can make decisions concerning your estate. However, in the case of a trust, you may be willing to transfer the duties of trustee to someone else, known as a successor trustee. As discussed earlier, if you only have a will, it may be necessary for a conservator to be appointed to manage your estate.

CHAPTER 7

BASIC ITEMS IN AN ESTATE PLAN

Many different items can be created within an estate plan, the simplest being a will. A will allows you to determine where your assets will go, and someone will be appointed to act as your executor in order to make sure your wishes are carried out. In most cases, a will is witnessed by several parties whose signatures must be notarized, and there are some other legal requirements associated with wills as well.

Another item that can be created within an estate plan is a revocable living trust, which is what most people consider the living trust. A revocable living trust can be changed in any way or revoked altogether while it is in place. Once you pass, however, most of the trust provisions become irrevocable and cannot be changed by the beneficiaries.

A power of attorney document is typically involved in an estate plan. This document is created in almost every case where a will is created, and it names a person who will handle your finances in the event that you become temporarily incapacitated. Other documents include the title that you will want to have transferred into the trust, deeds, and an advance directive or medical power of attorney.

In the event that you become unable to make your own health-related or medical decisions, an advance directive is a document that allows medical providers to know what your wishes would have been. For example, if you end up on life support, the medical providers will know whether you would have wanted to remain on life support or be removed from life support. Each state has its own forms and methods for the creation of advance directives.

CHAPTER 8

HOW TO SETTLE THE ESTATE WHEN SOMEONE PASSES AWAY?

Once someone passes away, their financial affairs will need to be handled, which typically involves paying for their burial and final bills, and ensuring that things are maintained during the transition phase and during the distribution of assets. In the case of a trust, the trustee would want to meet with the attorney who created the trust or an attorney of their choosing who can provide instructions as to what they should do first. Typically, it would involve deciding where to keep and how to handle the assets. In most cases, it will be stated in the trust where the personal items should go and whether they want the assets equally distributed or distributed in a specific way to certain beneficiaries.

Next, the trustee or executor will have to insure that the proper tax returns are prepared based on the income they earned up until the time of their death. In the case of a will or trust, this involves any income earned up until their death and, in many case, any income earned while the will or trust is being administered.

The final process involves ensuring that the assets are distributed according to the requirements of the trust. For instance, if there are any minor children, minor trusts, or other types of testamentary trusts, then it will need to be made sure that they are funded and administered correctly.

In many cases, an attorney is not required in order to administer and ultimately, distribute a trust. An attorney may be needed initially, but not for the entire process. When dealing with complex estates or large asset trusts that involve several legal and tax-related issues, an attorney will likely need to be involved. Trusts are designed to be a lot easier for a person to handle individually, without the need for an attorney. In many cases, a single meeting with an attorney will be sufficient to direct a person as to how to proceed.

Probate essentially refers to any assets owned by the individual at the time of their death that were not placed in a trust, such as real estate, stocks, or anything else in the decedent's name. The process of probate requires the executor or Personal Representative to ensure that the wishes of the will are followed, that creditors are paid, and that the taxes are handled properly. The personal representative will need to have a petition filed to probate the will. Most people will need an attorney to help them with that process, as it is fairly complex and rule-based. Very few probates can be handled without the services of an attorney and many states require a lawyer.

Once the death certificate and original will is obtained, probate will be filed for and the executor will be appointed. If it is stated in the will that there is no bond requirement, then a bond will not have to be created. However, if the will does not say anything about waiving a bond, then the personal representative must have the ability to obtain one. A bond is essentially an insurance policy that makes sure that the personal representative is managing the affairs correctly. Most wills waive the bond requirement, which means that the personal representative can serve without it.

Once the probate process has begun, notifications are sent to creditors, heirs, and to any other entities required by the particular state law. Following this, the process of administration begins. The personal representative will obtain and value the assets, which is a process sometimes assisted by the state. The personal representative will then file an inventory with the court that establishes the items in the estate.

On average, probate processes take between six and 10 months, but some states have a requirement as to how long probates must be opened in order to allow creditors to file claims. Creditors have to be paid in a certain order, and in some cases, there are so many debts in an estate that there is nothing left for the beneficiaries. In such cases, the personal representative's job is to make sure the creditors are paid, including credit companies, mortgage holders, and attorneys and accountants who are working on the estate.

Once the estate is completed, it is up to the personal representative and the attorney to complete an accounting. There are several different ways that can be done, but an accounting is a way for the court to make sure that everything has been handled correctly. Once the accounting is approved by the court (after beneficiaries are given time to object), the court will approve the distribution of assets to the beneficiaries.

Generally, people understand that the cost of probate is high because they need more expertise in the form of a lawyer for almost every comprehensive process that involves the court. Some states are slower at dealing with probates through the court system because they have a lower priority than criminal cases or other civil cases.

CHAPTER 9

WHAT IS A TRUST AS IT RELATES TO ESTATE PLANNING?

A trust is an arrangement that allows a third party or a trustee to hold assets on behalf of the beneficiary or beneficiaries, and it becomes effective the moment it is signed by the trustor. A trust is a way of avoiding the probate process and associated fees. It also allows the trustee to manage the assets during the life of the beneficiary. Since the initial trustee is usually the grantor as well, a successor trustee is the person or entity appointed in the trust to serve as the trustee upon the disability or death of the trustee and/or grantor. The concept of a trust is to transfer titles to some or all of the person's property to a trustee who holds the title in the trust for the benefit of the beneficiaries named within the trust.

The trustor (the person crating the trust) is the individual or organization that gives funds or assets to others by transferring fiduciary duty to a third-party trustee who will maintain the assets for the benefit of the beneficiary. The trustee is the individual or individuals giving control or powers of administration of the property and funds of the trust with the legal obligation to administer the trust solely for the purposes specified within the text of the trust. Co-trustees may come into play when several individuals manage a trust with equal control over the decisions and administration of the trust.

The beneficiary of the trust is the person who receives the benefit of the trust. In the case where the grantor is still alive and receiving the benefits of the trust, that person also counts as a beneficiary. Once that person dies, the people who are named as individuals entitled to assets or income from the trust (either immediately or over a period of time) are beneficiaries.

Most states have adopted the Uniform Trust Code, which is the model law for states to use for creating a comprehensive process for creating, interpreting, or administering trusts. This ensures some level of consistency with regard to how trusts are put together and administered on a state-by-state basis.

A revocable trust is created with the option of amending or revoking it, and is the most common type of trust. This is because it allows for flexibility in the face of changes with regard to family situations and tax and distribution laws. Most trusts are amended or restated rather than revoked in full. The trust document is what is usually amended or changed. On the other hand, an irrevocable trust cannot be revoked or amended. It is typically used when the grantor wants to ensure that the beneficiaries will receive the assets. It is also used in spendthrift or credit shelter trusts in order to protect assets from creditors or to take advantage of tax laws.

CHAPTER 10

CAN A TRUST AVOID PROBATE?

A trust can avoid probate due to the fact that the assets within it are passed on for the trustee to manage. Once that occurs, there is no need for the assets to be transferred according to the probate process. There may be situations in which the trust does not avoid probate due to the fact that the trust itself was not properly funded. A trust has to be funded by having assets transferred to the name of the trust, which may include stocks, bank accounts, homes, cars, and other things of that nature. If there is anything left out of the trust, then those assets may have to be probated into the trust.

Trusts include what is known as a pour-over will, which is a will that is done in conjunction with the trust and essentially acts as a "catchall". This means that if there are any assets that are not in the trust, those assets are to be probated and administered according to the trust terms. Generally, however, trusts are not subject to probate.

Are Assets Held In A Trust Protected From Creditors In All Cases?

In many cases, the assets that are held in a trust are not protected from creditors. For instance, in a revocable living trust, the trustor is responsible for paying their creditors. If they are sued or if there are any other claims of creditors, the trustee must pay the creditors.

There are certain circumstances in which a trust can protect beneficiaries from creditors, the most common of which is a spendthrift trust. In this type of trust, the money is passed to a beneficiary and is to be managed by a trustee in accordance with the terms of the trust. This means that creditors are disallowed from accessing the principal of the trust. In many circumstances, the creditors will have a right to the income that comes out of the trust and goes to the beneficiary, but they do not have a right to invade the trust principal.

A "special needs trust" operates similarly, and is set up under the law to allow someone to continue to obtain financial aid from the government without losing their inheritance. This type of trust has very specific instructions with which it must comply, and there are other maintenance requirements that prevent creditors from invading the trust.

If someone has a lot of money, they can create an irrevocable trust, but there is a cost associated with these trusts. In addition, they would be unable to act as the trustee or make any changes to the trust. As a result, most control over the assets is lost in order to ensure that the principal of the trust is protected from creditors. However, this does not mean that if they are subject to a big lawsuit or claim that they can automatically create an irrevocable trust. Most states have laws that categorize such actions as fraudulent or as wrongful transfers, and as a result, the state would have the power to undo the irrevocable trust and allow creditors to access it. In summary, only under certain circumstances are assets in a trust protected from creditors, and they are usually very complicated.

CHAPTER 11

IS A WILL AS GOOD AS A TRUST?

Depending upon your goals, a will may or may not be just as good as a trust. The former has the benefit of being less expensive and is typically easier to understand, and the probate process can actually be a positive by allowing you to ensure that a judge or someone is overlooking what takes place. While it may take longer and be more expensive, a probate affords you the security of having the court system involved, which frequently acts as a protective mechanism.

A trust, however allows you to avoid probate and the associated costs, as well as the risk of conservatorship.

As discussed earlier, a trust allows the individual trustee to distribute assets based on the instructions in the trust to the beneficiary. No court is involved. Additionally, a trust eliminates the need for a conservatorship (or other similar protective proceeding) since the successor trustee can take over administration of the property in the estate. This can act as a significant cost savings in addition to avoiding the very stressful process of involving courts in private affairs.

The disadvantage of trusts is that they are expensive and require more housekeeping in order to ensure that they are properly funded. If you have large amounts of money, then trusts can actually be easier to deal with in terms of protecting the assets from being taxed. It might be the case that a trust is more appropriate for you, but you may choose to go with a will for matters of simplicity. Alternatively, you may want to choose a more complex route, but doing so will necessitate an understanding of your goals and values. Ultimately, the decision to choose a will over a trust or vice versa is something that you should discuss with an attorney. Perhaps after reading this book and conducting your own research, you will be able to reach a joint decision.

CHAPTER 12

COMPONENTS OF AN EFFECTIVE TRUST

There are many components that comprise an effective trust, so it is best to hire an attorney to assist you. An attorney will understand the tax and trust laws, as well as be able to make it understandable for everyone. You do not need to have a 30 or 50-page trust in order to accomplish what's necessary; it could be done more accurately and clearly in a 10 or 15-page trust. In fact, I think that very good attorneys are able to use language in a more economical way and curtail things to what specifically you want.

The most important steps to developing a trust are determining who gets which assets, and how the trust will be administered. A trust should have very specific instructions for the trustee so that there is no confusion with regard to how the assets should be managed, what should and should not be invested, how they should treat the beneficiaries, and how to properly file taxes. It should also be made clear what the trustee cannot do, which includes keeping money for personal purposes, allowing beneficiaries to take out loans for themselves, and putting people in nursing homes without having the appropriate approval from the court.

There are several components that you may want to have in a trust, such as a no-contest clause, which states that if anyone unsuccessfully contests the trust, then their trust share should be reduced to zero. This is a measure that may be implemented in order to prevent frivolous litigation or unsubstantiated claims against the trust or trustee by beneficiaries.

Obligations Of The Trustee In Keeping Beneficiaries Updated On What Is Happening

A trustee has fiduciary duties, which are typically described in the trust or under state law. Essentially, a trustee owes a duty of good faith, loyalty, and fair dealings with the beneficiaries or anyone who is meant to benefit from the trust. This means that a trustee cannot act selfishly, but rather for the benefit of others. They cannot hide things from people, lie about the assets in a trust, or fail to pay creditors. They have the duty to handle the money as if it were their own.

In addition, the duties of the trustee are to ensure that the trust's responsibilities are followed, which means that if a beneficiary was left out of the trust, the trustee cannot just ignore that fact. Regardless of whether or not the trustee believes the trust to be fair in all regards, they must comply with it. The trustee is also required to comply with all state and federal tax laws, and cannot delegate their responsibilities to anyone else.

Of course, all of this is done with the help of the attorney who will explain to the trustee the nature of their responsibilities. If the trustee happens to be their client, then they need to make sure that they are complying with the requirements. Frequently, a breach of fiduciary duties is not an intentional act; sometimes it is negligent, or stems from a misunderstanding.

The personal representative of an estate that is being administered via a probate has the same responsibilities as a trustee, however, the court generally has the ability to supervise what is going on. Typically, personal representatives are required to establish and disclose to the court and accountant everything on which they've spent the money, paid creditors of the estate, or distributed to beneficiaries. In many cases, the personal representative must also gain approval to pay the attorney that is handling the trust out of the assets in the estate.

CHAPTER 13

ADVICE FOR CLIENTS WHO ARE AFRAID OF LOSING CONTROL OVER ASSETS IN A TRUST

When a client is afraid of losing control over their assets in a revocable or, in some cases, irrevocable trust, I tell them that having a trust of any kind will give them the best chance to ensure that their assets will be under the control of someone they trust. It is helpful if they have a friend or family member who they trust to handle their matters. If someone does not create a will or trust, then it is more likely that someone who they do not trust will be appointed to manage their assets, because the court could appoint a conservator. In addition, the person who would be appointed would more likely charge a fee.

I always tell people that it is important to let the person whom they appoint know that they have been appointed so that they are able to prepare emotionally and do some research on the responsibilities they'll be assuming. In general, I don't recommend leaving several people as co-trustees, because if they do not get along, then it can counter the needs of the trust. Sometimes people have a hard time choosing which of their children should be the trustee, because they do not want to be seen as choosing a "favorite." However, it is best to choose one person whom is trusted by the grantor and the beneficiaries.

Chapter 14

Should I Create More Than One Trust?

If you are considering having more than one trust, then you may consider having a testamentary trust, and whether or not that is the right choice for you will depend upon your circumstances. A testamentary trust exists within a primary trust or within a will, and insures that when you pass, your assets will go into another trust for the benefit of that beneficiary. It is the alternative to that beneficiary receiving all of the money at once.

These are common in situations where you have minor children inheriting money. Most people want the money to be managed in a separate trust until the children reach a certain age. This prevents the money from being spent all at once. Alternatively, you may want a charitable trust so that the money that remains after your beneficiary receives a certain amount will go to a charity.

There are many other reasons for why you may choose to have a testamentary trust, some of which include tax or investing purposes. If you are concerned about estate taxes and you have a large enough trust, then you could have a credit shelter trust, which would hold a certain amount of money that would go to your spouse and be protected from estate taxes. Upon the passing of your spouse, the assets would go to your children. This would protect the money from being spent in its entirety by your spouse, or from being used in any way not intended by the beneficiary.

There are also trusts designed to keep firearms or other property that is heavily regulated by the state or federal government, designed to prevent the complex process of transferring these assets to individuals.

If you have a child or a beneficiary who is subject to some type of handicap or other incapacity that requires them to receive federal benefits, then you may want to create a special needs trust within the trust. Doing so would allow you to reserve money within the trust solely for the purposes of caring for that beneficiary, rather than for housing, food, or anything else for which federal aid would provide. Special needs trusts are meant to provide for entertainment, travelling, and other purchases that would make the beneficiary's life more fulfilling.

A spendthrift trust is somewhat related to a special needs trust, and may be created if you have a beneficiary whom you want to ensure uses the money only in accordance with what the trustee dictates. A spendthrift trust also protects the body of the trust from being attacked by creditors. In most states, the income that goes to the beneficiary can be subject to creditors, but the body of the trust cannot.

CHAPTER 15

TRUSTS THAT WE HAVE NOT DISCUSSED YET

An IRA trust is also known as an IRA beneficiary trust, which is a separate trust used as a beneficiary of tax deferred IRA accounts or retirement accounts for estate planning purposes. Simply naming your trust itself as a beneficiary on your beneficiary designation is not advisable, because if you do that, then it will automatically count as a distribution for the purposes of the IRA, and will be immediately taxed. As a result, there will be significant impacts to the beneficiaries of your IRA. Instead, you can name a trust as a designated beneficiary for the IRA, and ensure that the trust includes certain stipulations that will prevent the IRA from immediately being taxed. In addition, it will allow for the IRA to be managed correctly by the beneficiaries, or a separate trustee, so that they do not make decisions that hurt them taxwise. In all cases, it is advisable to talk to a lawyer or a CPA concerning how to handle IRA's in your estate planning.

The IRA trust is a sub-trust that would be listed as a beneficiary of a person's IRA after their passing. In many cases, IRAs are protected from the claims of creditors while the IRA account holder is still living, and in many states, they protect retirement accounts from creditors as well. However, when the account holder passes, the IRA assets go in the individual beneficiary and the IRA is no longer protected. To counter this, IRA assets are passed into an IRA trust and protected from creditors' lawsuits and divorcing spouses, so long as the funds remain inside of the trust. This will ensure that the assets from the IRA remain there for use and benefit of the beneficiaries in the event that the beneficiary files for bankruptcy, gets sued, or gets married and later divorces.

The IRA trust can also protect the beneficiary from their own bad decisions, such as blowing all of the money on items unrelated to retirement. If an IRA is left directly to your beneficiaries instead of a trust. They can then cash out the IRA and spend the money as they see fit. If a beneficiary opts to cash out the IRA instead of leaving it in the trust, then all of the withdrawn money would be included as taxable income to the beneficiary for that year and could be subject to additional penalties. The taxes can be significant, sometimes higher that 50% in combined federal tax and penalties and state tax.

A separate problem with naming your beneficiary to an IRA would arise if the beneficiary is a minor. If this is the case, the minor cannot be the recipient of the IRA without a guardianship or a conservatorship in place, at least until the minor reaches the age of 18. To protect the IRA assets, the passing of an IRA trust means that the grantor can put limits and restrictions on how the IRA assets are to be spent and how much the beneficiary can withdraw.

Also, we have many people who want their animals to be taken care of after they pass. They therefore have the option in many states of creating a "pet trust". This legal arrangement determines who will take care of your pets once you die and how your pets' care will be funded. Households with higher incomes and larger families tend to include pets in their estate planning, because for many, they are known to be just as important as human children. Traditionally, state laws have not accommodated a pet owner who wants to provide for a pet's care after their passing or incapacitation, without having a trust. However, a direct gift of money or property to a pet is legally not possible because they are considered property, and a piece of property cannot hold title.

Regardless, in many states, a trust can be prepared for the benefit of one or more pets that are alive during and after the trustor's lifetime. A pet trust would terminate at the end of the life of the pet, and would go back to the alternate beneficiaries or to a successor beneficiary. A person who agrees to care for a pet may receive compensation from that trust for their efforts, and a person who has an interest in the welfare of an animal may request to be appointed by the court to become that animal's caretaker.

It's not uncommon to see disputes over pet trusts, especially from spurned beneficiaries. In some cases, the trustee may have to get the court involved if there are any disputes or questions as to what is supposed to happen to the money during the pet's lifetime. Because of this, it is very important that you make your desires very explicit, which typically requires the help of an attorney.

Another type of trust is known as a Medicaid trust, which are spend down or income cap trusts designed to preserve the trustor's assets in anticipation of a possible long-term disability. Medicaid trusts can sometimes be created in order to allow someone to qualify for state assistance. If you think you are going to be going into a nursing home, then you may be able to create a Medicaid trust so that you will be able to apply for Medicaid benefits without having to sell all of your assets. There are very specific rules as to who can qualify for these and something for which you will need to speak with a very experienced attorney.

Asset protections trusts are allowed in certain states, and you do not have to live within a particular state in order to create one. These types of trusts allow you have a trustee manage your money for your benefit as long as you do not have any control over what that person or institution is doing with your assets. In this way, these trusts can protect your assets because you really do not "own" them.

For instance, if you are concerned about the type of business you are in or the associated risks, then you may decide to have assets put into a certain type of a trust and appoint someone to manage it in the event that a large claim is made against you. With that said, this is not something that you can do in an attempt to escape current creditors, because doing so would be considered a fraudulent transfer. Creating these types of trusts is very tricky and specific, and therefore generally requires the assistance of an experienced attorney who understands the associated laws.

An irrevocable life insurance trust is an irrevocable and non-amendable trust. Upon the death of the insurer, the policy is invested into the trust, and the trustee then invests the insurance proceeds and administers it. If the beneficiary is reckless with money or you are otherwise concerned about the way in which they will use it, then you can create a life insurance trust that will be funded with the life insurance proceeds and administered according to the requirements of the trust.

CHAPTER 16

MORE INFORMATION ABOUT TRUST ADMINISTRATION

You may try to avoid probate by gifting property to your children or by putting your child's name on your house, stocks, or other pieces of property. This, however, is a very bad idea. It is much better to create a trust, because once you give away your money, you cannot get it back. For instance, if you were to give your money or house to your children and if they were to get sued, then your assets would be at risk and you would be unable to get them back.

There are also tax consequences that come along with this. Much of the income to the federal government is collected through the Capital Gains Tax. The idea of this is that if property is sold at a profit, you have to pay taxes on the profit.

A common term and factor in capital gains taxes is called a tax "basis". This is how much the property was purchased for. In many cases, the largest asset in an estate is real estate. Under current federal law, if you inherit property, the tax basis increases to the value established at the date of death. This means that when the beneficiary sells that property, they will only have to pay capital gains taxes based upon the difference between the date of death value and the date of selling value. However, if you were to gift your house to your children, then they are going to have to pay capital gains taxes, which can be as much as 40 percent in some states. In property that was purchased long ago and that has appreciated substantially, this can cost 10's of thousands of dollars in federal and state taxes.

You need to speak with your accountant and attorney before deciding to gift anything to anyone, and you don't want to use gifting as a way to avoid probate. I have met with many sophisticated clients who have either received poor advice in this regard, or have taken it upon themselves to research the topic online and make a decision without having considered all of the consequences. You should not make estate planning decisions based upon information that you find on the internet, from a paralegal, or from any company that just gives you documents. While you may save money doing this, there is a fairly good chance that you are going to do it wrong, which can result in substantial costs.

It is also important to speak with your bookkeeper, accountant, or your estate professional about the fact that you are creating a trust so that they can advise you as to which assets could be put into the trust. Make sure that you see a competent and experienced attorney who truly understands the consequences of poorly drafted trusts. I have done a lot of litigation work related to trust disputes and I am aware of these consequences, which allows me to write trusts in a way that prevents them from becoming an issue. In order to make the process easier for your lawyer, it is helpful to have all of the necessary documents available and in order, including your titles. Lastly, make sure that your trusts are properly funded.

CHAPTER 17

WHAT EXACTLY IS PROBATE?

Probate is a legal, statutory process by which you transfer property from a decedent to the decedent's beneficiaries. There are essentially two main types of probate, one of which is called intestate probate. Intestate probate occurs when a person dies without a will and has property that must go through the probate process. Every state has its own system, but in general, the probate process ensures that all creditors are paid, that anyone who has any legal claims are dealt with, and that assets are distributed to the beneficiaries according to the instructions in the will.

The process is started when the executor of the estate files a petition with the court to probate the will, and is almost always done with the assistance of an attorney.

The executor of an intestate estate (an estate where there is no will) has to be someone who is interested in the affairs of the estate, which means it can be a creditor, a family member, or in certain circumstances, it can be a friend. The executor petitions for probate and typically has to post a bond, which is essentially an insurance instrument meant to ensure performance of the executor. Once that is done and the probate is filed, the court will usually start the probate by signing the order appointing the executor as the actual person responsible for the probate in a will.

The executor will collect and obtain all of the assets, which will require them to search the decedent's bank records to identify their assets. They may have to go into a bank account or safe deposit box or any safe that the decedent may have had in order to obtain all the asset information. They are then required to account to the court everything that they find, which in most states is done by filing an inventory with the court. Certain assets do not have to be probated, such as those on which the decedent's name is with someone else's name. For instance, if there is a co-owner on a bank account, then that co-owner is entitled to the entire account.

Life insurance policies typically have named beneficiaries to which they automatically go. In the rare case that there is no beneficiary listed in the life insurance policy, the life insurance proceeds go to the executor to distribute according to the terms of the will. There is also a process by which creditors can exercise their right to pursue claims against the estate. Some creditors are state departments of human services that provided certain benefits to the decedent prior to their death. If someone has a lawsuit against or is owed money by the decedent, they will have to file a claim. The executor is required to notify all creditors of the probate, and in most states, they are also required to publish the probate in a paper of general circulation so that creditors have the chance to make their claim for the money owed.

Once everything has been done and the tax returns have been filed, distribution of the estate will occur. This typically involves the executor filing a final account that lists all of the assets and expenses of the estate. In many cases, they have to show that tax returns have been filed. Once that is completed and there are no objections to the accounting filed by any creditors or heirs, they can file a petition with the court to have the assets of the estate distributed in accordance with the will. After creditor's claims, administrative claims, medical bills, and the legal fees of doing the estate are paid, the remaining balance is paid to the beneficiaries.

CHAPTER 18

MISCONCEPTIONS ABOUT THE PROBATE PROCESS

Since it is more expensive to do a probate than it is to administrate trust, many people think that their estate is just going to be spent on legal fees. Another misconception is that probate requires paying more taxes, but that is simply not true; trusts and probates have the same tax issues to the extent of the size of the estate or any other type of income tax. Many people also have the misconception that probate takes much longer than a trust administration, which is usually only the case if there are legal disputes between heirs, tax issues, contests of the trust or the will, or any other type of litigation. However, the large majority of them take less than a year.

There are reasons to avoid the probate process, but there are benefits as well. If a case involves contentious children and there is no one who can be trusted as a trustee, then it may be better to do probate and have the court supervise the process. In addition, having a will during one's lifetime requires less work in terms of keeping everything organized, because the heirs would deal with that one the person has passed. Trusts are advisable for people who have average to significant amount of assets.

Is Probate Necessary?

Probate is not necessary if the person does not have any assets that are subject to probate. For instance, if they did not own real estate or if their bank accounts were in survivorship and there are no assets, then probate would not be necessary. If the amount of assets is below a certain level, then there is a different process that can be used. Every state is different, but if there is a statutory process, then it is an alternative to what there would be in a formal probate. In a trust circumstance, there are generally no probates involved if everything has been funded correctly. If real property is jointly owned in survivorship, then it is very unlikely that there would be a need for probate. Instead, the assets would likely go to the remaining spouse or beneficiaries.

If a case involves children from different marriages, then it is very important that everyone is on the same page in order to ensure that the children are treated essentially the same in both estate plans. That is fairly complex, but it is something that can be worked through with the help of an attorney. Complicated and contentious probates often involve children from different marriages who do not trust each other, and this can lead to conflict and litigation.

CHAPTER 19

FACTORS THAT SET THE STAGE FOR A PROBATE TO OCCUR

If someone died without a will or trust and they had property, then probate will occur. If they had a will but no trust, probate will still occur. If they had a trust but they did not leave everything in the trust that they were supposed to, then there would have to be a probate of those assets into the trust. This is why it is important that trusts are properly funded. If someone buys a house or car, it's important that they let the title company know about it so that the property can be put into the trust. It is also important to make sure that bank accounts are in a trust. Probate will also be triggered by wrongful death claims. For instance, if the decedent is run over in a car accident because of negligence, then their executor would have to file a wrongful death claim, and they would have to go through the probate process. This is true whether or not the decedent had a trust.

What Are My Options For Avoiding Probate?

The most common way of avoiding probate is to do a trust, because there is no requirement for the property in a trust to go through the court supervised probate process. Another way of avoiding probate is by having property owned in survivorship with a spouse. Lastly, probate will not be necessary if someone has no property.

CHAPTER 20

MORE INFORMATION ABOUT PROBATE PROCESS

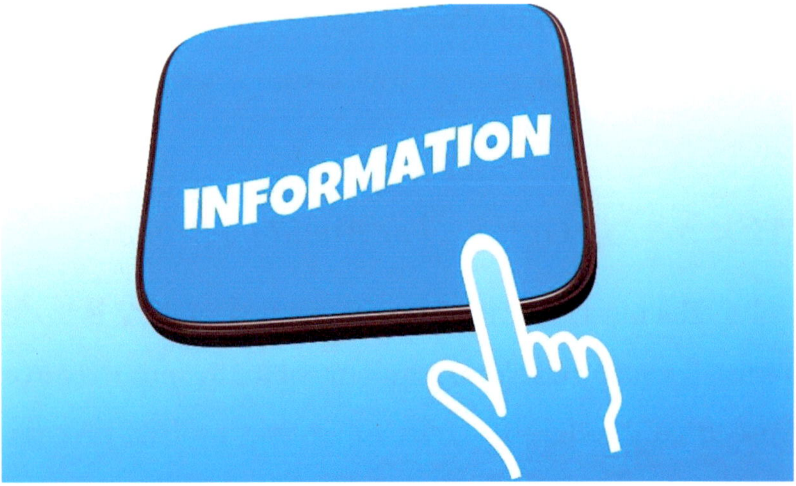

When dealing with the probate process, it is important that you ensure that all creditors get paid. In certain circumstances and in certain states, failing to properly handle the estate may result in the Personal Representative or Executor being held responsible for paying the obligation, which is especially true when taxes are owed to the government.

One benefit of probate is the issue of "barred claims", which exists in almost every state. If a creditor has not made a claim and they were not a known creditor within a certain period of time, then their claim would be barred. In fact, if anyone who felt they were owed money by you did not file a claim within a certain period of time, then they would never be able to claim that money. If a claim is filed within the appropriate timeframe, then it would be up to the executor to decide whether to approve or deny that claim. If the claim is denied, then that person could seek the assistance of the court in obtaining what they believe to be owed.

Statute Of Limitations For Filing A Claim

In many states, there are statute of limitations for filing a creditor's claim typically around four months after the notice of publication of the claim. If they fail to file the claim (unless the claim is already known by the Personal Representative), then that claim is barred. Also, the Personal Representative can deny the claim if the Personal Representative believes it is invalid. That generally would require the creditor to seek court action to get the bill paid.

CHAPTER 21

HOW LONG DOES IT TAKE FOR A PROBATE CASE TO CONCLUDE?

Depending upon the state in which it's occurring, a probate case can take anywhere from seven months to three years or more to run its course. Probate cases are typically finished within a year if they are fairly straightforward and there are no complications and no need for litigation. If a significant amount of taxes must be paid, requiring the liquidation of property, then a case may take significantly longer. If someone wants to challenge some provisions in the will or claim that certain provisions in the will are invalid or unclear, then it could take longer.

I am currently handling a case that involves a homemade will that includes unclear language which would otherwise dictate the amount of assets each beneficiary would receive. The case is in the Oregon Court of Appeals and is awaiting a decision. This is just one example of why a case may take longer to get resolved.

The competency of the executor and his or her counsel will also affect the length of a probate case. If the executor is represented by competent counsel, then the process will be relatively simple for the executor, because their lawyer will generally be able to make court appearances and handle all of the legal filings. This can greatly shorten the process. However, there are usually factors outside of the executor's control that can require probate to take longer.

CHAPTER 22

CAN YOU HANDLE A PROBATE WITHOUT AN ATTORNEY?

Only in the rarest of circumstances can someone handle a probate without the assistance of an attorney. For instance, if they happen to be an estate attorney themselves and are probating an estate for their parents or loved ones, then they wouldn't need the assistance of another lawyer. The process is extremely time-consuming, and the risk of doing something improperly is high if there is no attorney there to assist. In fact, a person would probably end up spending more money in terms of the time spent attempting to do it themselves than they would on paying an attorney for assistance. In addition, if the correct court guidelines are not followed, then the court can remove the executor and appoint someone else to take their place. If the beneficiaries do not feel as though they are being treated fairly, then they may hire an attorney who would try to remove the executor.

While there is no legal requirement to have an attorney help with the probate process in most states, I have rarely met an individual who went through the process by themselves without making errors, some of which require paying out of pocket due to the improper filing of taxes. In other cases, a person will have already made so many mistakes by the time that they finally decide to hire a lawyer, that it will cost even more just to fix those problems. In summary, it is very unwise to handle a probate without an attorney.

INDEX

NOTES

Made in the USA
Monee, IL
05 November 2026

67385060R00052